THE LITTLE BOOK OF

# CANDLES

# THE LITTLE BOOK OF
# CANDLES

*A Guide to Styling Your Space,*
*Setting Your Intention,*
*and Illuminating Your Life*

DEVON FREDERICKSEN

DRIVEN

Published in the United States by Driven, an imprint of Zeitgeist™, a division of Penguin Random House LLC, New York.

penguinrandomhouse.com

ISBN: 9780525617617

Book design by Rachel Marek
Illustrations by Sam Michaels

Printed in the United States of America

1  3  5  7  9  10  8  6  4  2

Image credits: (AS: Adobe Stock / SS: Shutterstock) Cover (main), soul_studio / SS; Cover (left flame), IMG Stock Studio / SS; Cover (right flame), New Africa / SS; Cover (texture), YamabikaY / SS; ii, Atlas / AS; viii, anna.stasiia / AS; 3, Tayfun / AS; 5, frank p. neuhaus / AS; 6, victorgrigas via Wikimedia Commons; 8, MartaKlos / AS; 16, dk_photo / AS; 18, Prisca Laguna / SS; 19 (top), Design Pics Inc / Alamy Stock Photo; 19 (bottom), tj_armer / AS; 22, New Africa / AS; 29, Nata / AS; 30, New Africa / AS; 33, Soy + Cedar; 34, New Africa / AS; 37, New Africa / AS; 38, Annalisa / AS; 44, Daria Minaeva / AS; 47, Brittany / AS; 48, Africa Studio / AS; 50, agneskantaruk / AS; 51, EkaterinaKiseleva / AS; 53, Maya Kruchancova / AS; 54, NiceAndKnotted / Etsy; 56, Alena Ozerova / AS; 58, dimaris / AS; 61, Floral Deco / AS; 62, Daria Minaeva / AS; 65, Jeff Wasserman / Stocksy United; 66, Daria Minaeva / AS; 73, kichigin19 / AS; 75, Rawf8 / AS; 77, t0m15/ AS; 80, Sergio Hayashi / AS; 82, Yakobchuk Olena / AS

# CONTENTS

# INTRODUCTION

C andles hold special power. A single lit candle can animate a space, reset your frame of mind, and transform the tone of an occasion. Candlelight can instantly make a home feel warm, cozy, and inviting; a room feel intimate and moody; and a table feel festive and fun.

Versatile and practical, candles can be used for relaxation, remembrance, and romance. They set the appropriate mood for special occasions and ritualistic activities, from candlelit dinners and spa days to meditation practices and yoga sessions. Candles mark milestones like birthdays, anniversaries, and weddings; honor loved ones who have died; make celebrations and holidays feel more festive; and symbolize the sacred in religious ceremonies.

Across cultures, religions, and literature, candles have long held symbolic significance. In Shakespeare's *Macbeth*, a candle represents the impermanence of life. For Buddhists, candles signify respect and deference. During Day of the Dead celebrations, the flames of candles symbolize hope and faith.

This little book of candles will illuminate your knowledge on scent throw, wax ethics, burn time, and the appeal and use of various candle shapes and sizes. You'll learn about the historical origins of candlemaking, how to make your own candles, and how to incorporate candles into everyday life. You'll gain confidence in how to arrange the perfect candle display for different occasions and room designs, along with how to make candle crafts for holidays, celebrations, and gifts. To experiment with a bit of candle enchantment, you'll learn simple magic spells for getting what you want out of life and which candle colors to use for setting intentions. You'll learn how to integrate candles into daily rituals, which scents to use to snuff out a bad mood, and how different cultures and religions link candles to spiritual practices.

So, get comfy, light a candle, and read on.

# THE HISTORY OF
# CANDLES

*From Reeds to Tea Lights*

"How far that little candle throws his beams! So shines a good deed in a naughty world."

—WILLIAM SHAKESPEARE

For more than five thousand years in recorded human history, candles have provided a source of light for homes, celebrations, rituals, and religious ceremonies. Over the centuries, as candles around the world evolved, they have been made from a range of materials, including plants, insects, whale oil, rice, tree nuts, flax, pitch, and the fruit of cinnamon trees. The earliest candles may have been used by the ancient Egyptians, who constructed torches by soaking the core of reeds with liquified animal fat, or tallow. However, these torches were made without a wick, so they lacked an essential component that we associate with the modern-day candle.

The first candle with a wick is credited to the ancient Roman Empire, whose people dipped rolled papyrus in tallow or beeswax. These candles were

used as a source of light in homes, as torches for nighttime travelers, and as symbolic aids for religious rituals. And in ancient Greece, once a month, people celebrated the birth of Artemis, the lunar goddess, by making round cakes to represent the moon. The cakes were decorated with lit candles, the smoke sending prayers up to the gods.

In ancient China, candles were made from whale fat. Later, Chinese candlemakers made wax from a combination of insects and seeds, and they crafted wicks from rice paper.

The majority of early Western cultures primarily used tallow candles until the Middle Ages, when European countries began making candles from beeswax. This was an upgrade, since beeswax burns cleanly and smells mildly sweet, unlike tallow, which yields an unpleasant, abrasive odor. However, because of the price of beeswax candles, only the wealthy could afford them. By the thirteenth century, candlemaking had become a guild craft in England and France, and candlemakers (or chandlers) traveled door-to-door selling candles and collecting reserved kitchen fats for candle production.

In colonial times in America, women discovered that bayberry bushes produced berries that could be processed into sweet-smelling, clean-burning wax. However, given the extremely time-consuming way in which the wax had to be extracted from the berries, this method eventually fell out of favor.

By the sixteenth century, German households had begun adorning Christmas trees with candles. However, in those days, Christmas trees were only kept lit for about thirty minutes, during which constant attention had to be paid and buckets of water and sand kept on hand. Christmas tree fires eventually became so common that insurance companies wouldn't pay out for house fires caused by Christmas tree candles.

The first well-documented birthday cake was that of Count Ludwig von Zinzendorf in Germany in 1746. For his extravagant birthday celebration,

there was a large cake—as big as the town's largest oven could fit—decorated with the number of candles corresponding to his age.

In the late eighteenth century, the whaling industry introduced spermaceti, wax made from crystallized sperm-whale oil. When burned, this wax produced a bright light without tallow's off-putting odor. Similar to beeswax, however, spermaceti was expensive and therefore only available to those who could afford it.

Mass-produced candles were first manufactured by Joseph Morgan in 1834, when he invented a machine that could continuously produce molded candles. With that, affordable candles became more widely available.

Candlemaking began to decline after 1879, following the introduction of the light bulb. But by the end of the first half of the twentieth century, candles were gaining renewed popularity because the by-products of the oil and meatpacking industries had become a reliable source of paraffin and stearic acid, two ingredients used in candlemaking. By the mid-1980s, candles had become available in a broad range of colors, scents, shapes, sizes, and materials. They had also become more widely used as mood-setters, decorations, and gifts. By the 1990s, chemists were developing new, vegetable-based waxes from soy and palm oils.

Today, candles are more popular than ever and regularly incorporated into daily rituals, home décor, and celebrations.

# CHOOSING YOUR
# CANDLES

*Waxes, Wicks, and Shapes*

"Great fire leaps from the smallest spark."

—DANTE

W hich candles burn the longest? What are the ethics of candle wax? Which candles have the strongest scent? With so much to consider, selecting the right candle—or candle-making materials—can feel the opposite of Zen. But familiarizing yourself with the main components of a candle can shed light on a world of possibilities and help shift your mindset from noggin-scratching to knowledgeable.

When selecting candles, you'll want to think about wax and wick types, as well as candle shape. Wax type affects flame quality, burn time, and fragrance strength. The wick's size and material also contribute to burn time and burn cleanliness. The wick is the candle's fuel: too little fuel, and the candle can sputter out; too much, and the flame can flare or emit soot. Candle shape is another factor to consider, as each one is optimal for different uses.

Ultimately, it's the combination of wax, wick, and container that creates the overall experience of any candle. A good tactic is to store a variety of candles for different occasions, rooms, and moods. Here is a breakdown of widely available wax, wick, and candle types to help guide you.

# Waxes

## PARAFFIN WAX

Also known as *mineral wax*, paraffin wax is the most widely used wax in the candle industry because it's inexpensive, yields a high volume of fragrance, and holds its color well. Its various melting points also make it a versatile wax for different candle types, including pillars and container candles.

### What it is

Paraffin is a petroleum-based wax created from crude oil, a nonrenewable resource. It's nontoxic and clean-burning, although it can produce soot. Paraffin wax is sometimes combined with other chemicals or additives, but most researchers agree that chemical exposure from burning these candles doesn't pose a serious health risk.

### When to use it

A paraffin candle is best when you're on a budget. Paraffin also has good scent throw, so if high fragrance is what you're after, paraffin can provide that extra punch.

## SOY WAX

Clean- and slow-burning, as well as nontoxic, soy wax comes from a renewable resource and has good scent throw. Soy wax can sometimes be difficult for candlemakers to work with because of its finicky reaction to temperature.

### What it is

Soy wax is made from either 100 percent soybean oil or a combination of soybean oil and other products.  Soybean oil is extracted from soybeans by solvent or mechanical press, and then a hydrogen solution solidifies it into wax.

Soy wax doesn't require chemical amplifiers to hold scent well. But its scent throw isn't as strong as paraffin's because soy is denser and requires more heat to burn, so scent releases more slowly.

### When to use it

Soy wax is an affordable alternative to fossil fuel–derived paraffin wax because it burns slowly. It's also a versatile wax that can be used to make many candle types.

## BEESWAX

Classic and timeless, beeswax is one of the oldest types of candle wax and gives off a bright flame with a subtle, honey-like aroma. It offers the longest, cleanest burn of any candle wax. It's also a natural air purifier.

### What it is

Beeswax comes from honeybees and is a by-product of the honey-making process.

### When to use it

Beeswax is a good choice for people who are environmentally conscious. Many beeswax candles are unscented, making them an option for anyone sensitive to fragrance. Harder than other waxes, beeswax is great for pillar candles. When burned, beeswax produces negative ions that attach to positive ions in the air like mold and pollen, pulling these particles to the floor, and thereby cleaning the air.

Although usually more expensive than paraffin or soy candles, beeswax candles are the slowest-burning option, so you get the most bang for your buck.

## COCONUT WAX

Although usually the most expensive option, coconut wax is produced from a high-yield and sustainable resource, is clean-burning, and holds fragrance and color well.

### What it is

Made from cold-pressed coconut meat, coconut wax is often combined with soy wax to strengthen a candle's firmness.

Coconut crops are high yield, are rapidly renewable, and don't require the use of pesticides, making coconut wax a sustainable option.

### When to use it

Coconut wax boasts optimal scent throw and a long burn time. Plus, its colorless quality makes it easy to dye. So, this wax makes colorful, fragrant candles that burn slowly.

## The Science of Candles

A single candle is powered by a number of scientific processes. A candle's flame melts the wax, which vaporizes and releases hydrocarbons that react with oxygen to produce hydrogen and carbon dioxide. This chemical reaction produces light and heat, along with water vapor in the form of steam (made from the blue part of the flame) and smoke (made from the yellow part of the flame). The more clean-burning and pure the wax, the less smoke a candle produces. The wick serves as a steady fuel pump, pulling the pooled liquified wax into the flame to generate a continual burn.

## WAX BLENDS

A mix of different types of wax, blends are often used to produce candles that burn well.

### What they are

Often, wax blends are a mix of different waxes, combined to create a superior candle that uses the most beneficial quality of each kind of wax. Whichever wax type comprises the majority of the candle is usually the wax listed on the product. For example, a candle crafted from 51 percent coconut wax would be labeled as a "coconut blend."

### When to use them

Wax blends should be used when specific candle attributes are desired. For example, candles made from a blend of palm wax and coconut wax create a product with a strong burn and good scent throw.

## WAX ALTERNATIVES

### Gel candles

Gel candles are made from petroleum-based wax or synthetic hydrocarbons. They burn more than twice as long as wax candles and give off a unique, rich glow.

## *The Ethics of Candles*

Different candle waxes come from different sources. As noted earlier, paraffin comes from a nonrenewable resource. Soy wax is derived from a renewable resource, but the soybean industry has been cited as contributing to significant deforestation and the use of fertilizers and pesticides that contaminate soil and waterways. Once thought to be a sustainable option for candlemaking, palm wax is a by-product of the palm industry, which, as a result of the high global demand for palm products, has resorted to unsustainable growing practices, making palm wax a controversial option.

It's always best to research candle or wax manufacturers first before purchasing candles to make sure your purchase aligns with your values.

### Liquid candles

For the longest burn, opt for liquid candles, which can burn for thirty-five to forty hours. Usually made from palm or coconut oil, the mix of oils reduces soot. These candles can also be refilled with more liquid wax or cartridges.

### Flameless candles

To prevent fire hazards entirely, use flameless candles, which are perfect for windy outdoor weddings or settings with high fire danger. Either electronic or battery operated, flameless candles can produce a convincing candle-flicker effect. Given their small batteries, flameless candles should be kept out of reach of children.

# *Wicks*

### FLAT WICKS

The most common wick type, flat wicks are typically knitted together using three bundles of fiber, which will produce a consistent burn. With a flat wick, the flame will also curl, which allows the wick to trim itself, helping to reduce carbon buildup.

### SQUARE WICKS

Stronger and more rounded than flat wicks, square wicks are often used for beeswax candles because they help prevent the wick from clogging. Square wicks also produce a curled, self-wicking flame.

### CORED WICKS

Cored wicks are braided or knitted and use a stiff core material like tin, paper, zinc, or cotton that keeps the wick upright. Cored wicks are often used in votives, jar candles, devotional candles, and pillars.

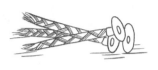

## WOODEN WICKS

Creating an earthy aesthetic, wooden wicks produce a crackling sound while they burn. They can be made from 100 percent wood or a mixture of wood and fibrous materials such as cotton. They can be single ply, multilayered, or curved.

## SPECIALTY WICKS

Certain wicks are designed for specific candle types, such as insect-repelling candles or oil lamps, and are manufactured for their particular burn qualities.

## How to Get the Most Out of Your Candles

Before any candle's first burn, read the instructions on the candle's packaging for recommendations. As a general rule, the first time it's lit, a new candle should burn for one hour for every one inch of the candle's diameter. For example, a candle with a two-inch diameter should burn for two hours the first time it's used. The first burn creates the "memory ring," which is the path the melted wax will follow for the life of the candle. Creating too small of a memory ring will cause the wax to melt in a narrow tunnel during each subsequent use.

Extend the life of any candle by trimming the wick to ¼ inch before each use. Long wicks can cause candle flames to flare or, when left crooked, to drip or burn unevenly. To increase the life of a candle up to 25 percent, trim the wick after every couple of hours of burn time.

Before lighting a candle, remove any debris left in the memory ring because additional material in the wax can cause the flame to flare up.

Don't burn a candle longer than the manufacturer's recommendation. Letting a candle go too long can cause the wick to "mushroom," which can lead to the flame flaring or releasing smoke and soot. As a rule of thumb, never burn a candle longer than four hours, making sure to cool the candle for at least two hours between each use.

To prevent black spots from developing on the side of a glass candle container, avoid burning a candle in an area with a lot of moving air, such as near open windows or fans or in crowded places.

Store candles in a cool, dry, dark location and cover with a lid. Ultraviolet rays from the sun can discolor candles. Scented candles have a life span of about six to twelve months, after which the fragrance weakens.

## Shapes

### TEA LIGHTS
Inexpensive and quick-burning, tea lights are small inch-high candles that sit in metal or plastic cups. Originally, they were used to keep teapots warm. Now, they are most commonly lit for soft mood lighting, religious ceremonies, heating scented oil, or keeping fondue warm.

### VOTIVES
Unlike tea lights, these short candles (about two inches tall) are made without a cup, meaning they must be placed in a container or on a dish so that the wax has somewhere to collect or drip. Votives make

a subtle statement with maximum ambience; they're a wonderful dinner table alternative to tall tapered candles, which can obscure dinner guests' views and overrun a table arrangement.

### TAPERS
Around since 3000 BC, tapers are classic. These elegant candles are tall and slender and taper to a soft point near the wick. They're an inexpensive option

for dining room table arrangements and for setting a romantic mood. Because of their skinny profile, taper candles are best placed in areas of focus. To reduce taper-candle drip, source tapers made with quality, dense wax. Keep tapers as straight as possible in their holders because any leaning can cause excess drip.

Trouble with tippy tapers? Use wax buttons: just knead to soften and then line your candleholders with them. No more tipping and dripping!

## PILLARS

As their name suggests, pillar candles are often cylindrical and tall (although they can also be square), and they are wider in diameter than taper candles.

They can stand alone without a container, but it's a good idea to burn them on a flame-resistant surface, like a plate or pillar candleholder, to catch any dripping wax. With a long-lasting burn, pillar candles are perfect for outdoor patio gatherings that stretch into the evening.

## Notes on Safety

- Never leave a candle unattended.

- Never use water to extinguish a candle; water can crack a hot glass container or cause melted wax to splatter.

- Don't touch or move a candle while it's burning.

- Keep candles out of reach of children and pets.

- Never burn a candle near flammable objects such as curtains, books, paper, bedding, decorations, or Christmas trees.

- Never burn a candle down all the way. For container candles, extinguish the flame when ½ inch of the base remains. For pillar candles, extinguish the flame when two inches of the base is left.

- Extinguish a candle flame if it stretches too high or flickers too much.

- Never light a candle if you might fall asleep.

## FLOATING

Normally two to three inches in diameter, these calming candles are specifically made to float in water. Their round  shape and short stature allow them to displace more water than their weight. With their glow flickering on the surface of the water, floating candles create a relaxing, romantic ambience, and they can be placed in bathtubs, stemware, bowls, and pools. Set them into the water by gently holding the wick, taking care not to get it wet. For outdoor gatherings, create a firepit feel by placing an abundance of floating candles in a large bowl or vase.

## BIRTHDAY

Birthday candles come in all sorts of shapes—spirals, stars, letters, numbers, animals, flowers, and more. Usually made with nontoxic paraffin wax, birthday candles can be arranged on cakes (or other  foods) for celebratory occasions. The most traditional style is a small, short taper that comes in different colors. Trick candles are also an option, with a self-light feature that's triggered after the candle has been blown out. For added impact, use sparkler birthday

# Making Candles at Home

*What you'll need:*

- Prewaxed, pretabbed wicks
- Hot glue gun and glue sticks
- Clean and dry candle containers (heatproof glasses, jars, teacups, tins, or old candle containers cleaned with simmering water)
- Masking tape or craft sticks
- Measuring cup
- Water
- Wax flakes or pellets
- Saucepan or heatproof glass pitcher
- Scale
- Pot (to use as double boiler)
- Mixing spoon
- Candy thermometer
- Fragrance (optional)
- Color (optional)

---

1. **Cover the surface** of your work area with a brown paper bag or newspaper.

2. Calculate the **volume of wax** you'll need by filling all the candle containers with water, then pouring this water into a liquid measuring cup. Note the volume; this is how much wax you'll need to melt. Dry the containers.

3. **Place a wick** in each candle container. **Adhere the wick** to the bottom of the container using a hot glue gun.

**4** **Cut a hole** in the middle of a piece of masking tape (the section of tape should be longer than the diameter of the candle container). **Insert the wick** through the hole and  press the masking tape down on either side of the container. Alternatively, use craft sticks to hold the wick in place.

**5** Place your melting pot on the **scale, tare it, and pour** in the required amount of wax flakes or pellets. For soy wax, 1 ounce of wax yields approximately 1 fluid ounce. For beeswax, 1 ounce of wax yields approximately 1.25 fluid ounces.

**6** **Heat the wax** in a double boiler over the heat source. Bring a pot of water to a gentle simmer, place a saucepan directly in the water, and heat the wax in the saucepan until melted (around 180°F).

**7** Wait until the wax has cooled to around 140°F before adding **color and/or fragrance** to the

wax (optional). Use a ratio of 1 ounce of fragrance for every 1 pound of wax.

8. Carefully **pour the melted wax** into the candle container.

9. Once the wax has cooled completely, **trim the wick** to ¼ inch.

**Note:** Candlemaking can be a finicky process with mixed results. Play around with fragrances, container sizes, and wicks until you discover your preferred method. You'll know if you need to adjust your wick size if the candle produces soot (wick is too thick) or if the melted pool of wax doesn't extend to the sides of the container (wick is too thin). Adjust on your next batch!

candles, which crackle and glitter in an impressive, entertaining display.

## CONTAINER CANDLES/CANDLE POTS

A container candle is poured directly into a non-flammable container. Container candles can also

contain more fragrance than freestanding candles, given the lower melting point. Because they're self-contained, these candles don't drip. Once the candle has burned through, most containers can be cleaned and reused.

## TRAVEL CANDLES

These candles are poured into a compact travel-size tin with a lid. The lid offers a built-in way to extinguish the candle, and the small size and non-breakable container make these candles perfect for tucking into your luggage for a relaxing getaway.

## SEVEN-DAY CANDLES

Often used for religious rituals and spiritual ceremonies or to adorn shrines, these candles are made from colored wax poured into a tall, cylindrical glass container, often decorated with religious motifs. Slow-burning, seven-day candles are intended to be burned continuously for seven days, although they can be used for shorter intervals. If you do burn the candle for its namesake period, make sure to place the candle in a low-risk area like a fireplace, bathtub, or sink to minimize fire hazards. Before lighting

a seven-day candle, it's standard to set an intention. After the candle has burned for a little while, note the color of the soot for spiritual implications. If the candle produces black soot, this can symbolize inner negativity. White soot represents a pathway for spiritual cleansing.

## Upcycling Containers

Once your container candle burns down, you don't need to throw away that lovely candle pot. You can upcycle it into a holder for trinkets, cotton swabs, paper clips, and more. To remove leftover wax, place the candle pot in the freezer until the wax is frozen, then pry the wax disc out with a butter knife. To remove any wax residue in the candle pot, boil water in a kettle, then pour it into the candle pot. The bits of wax will float to the top. Very carefully, dump the water out before it cools completely.

SETTING THE
# MOOD

*The Psychology of Lighting,
Candle Colors for the Moment,
and Setting the Scent*

"Look at how a
single candle can
both defy and
define darkness."

—ANNE FRANK

## The Psychology of Lighting

L ighting can quite literally set a mood! Variations in light trigger the brain to respond according to biological predispositions. For example, low light generates feelings of intimacy and restfulness, whereas brighter light stimulates the mind and intensifies emotions. A candle's flame provides a peaceful ambience that helps the body unwind and relax. If your mind associates candles with being a source of light in the darkness, candles can spark regenerative feelings of hope and vitality. Simply being in the proximity of warm lighting can make you feel warmer.

To achieve the desired mood, use candles alone or with other light sources to produce just the right lighting. For example, for romantic occasions like anniversaries, Valentine's Day, or date nights, position red pillar candles in varying heights around a room to cast the space in an intimate glow. Space out tea lights or votives in the bathroom to encourage relaxation. Place floating candles in the bath for a warm light that will help you feel cozy. Outdoor torch candles amp up the atmosphere of an alfresco get-together.

Tapered candles paired with low levels of room light set an elegant mood. Brightly colored, bold candles with a thick flame can add energy to festive gatherings.

## Candle Colors for the Moment

Even when unlit, candles can add to the ambience of a space. In interesting pots and holders, and with waxes in countless hues, they are part of a space's décor. Use the psychology of colors to infuse a room with intent or to set a mood for a special occasion. Soothing or neutral colors are best for office spaces and bathrooms. Rich colors work well in bedrooms and living rooms. Gold and silver candles are perfect for sparkly events like New Year's Eve. Try red anywhere you'd like to add a little romance or purple for a pop of power where you need it most.

Swap out colors to signal the change in seasons. Rejuvenating colors like green and blue can celebrate the arrival of spring. Energizing colors like orange and yellow can herald the coming of summer. Autumnal colors like orange, red, and purple make fall feel festive. (You can throw in black candles for Halloween.) Winter calls for white and green, with red or blue accents (depending on the holiday).

| Color | Represents |
|---|---|
| Red | Love, passion, intensity, romance, comfort, courage, friendship, protection, sexuality, heart |
| Pink | Kindness, faithfulness, affection, goodness |
| Orange | Creativity, excitement, happiness, warmth, prosperity, change, support |
| Yellow | Cheer, sun, energy, laughter, optimism, clarity, abundance, charisma, self-assurance |
| Green | Nature, growth, wealth, harmony, health, security, fertility, ambition, luck, youth, beauty |
| Blue | Calmness, tranquility, water, sky, truth, air, wisdom, confidence, trust, flexibility, healing |
| Purple | Pride, power, luxury, magic, dignity, mystery, independence, enlightenment |
| Black | Death, strength, formality, elegance, prestige, mourning, psychic protection |
| White | Purity, innocence, neutrality, cleanliness, beginnings, safety, faith, peace, sincerity, serenity |
| Brown | Physical healing, animal wisdom, grounding, home |
| Gold | Attraction, compassion, solar magic |

## Setting the Scent

Just as light affects the brain, so, too, does scent. Aromatherapy is the medicinal use of scents to heal the mind, body, and spirit. Scents send powerful signals, activating the limbic system, which is the part of the brain where memories are stored. Inhaling the right fragrance can cause a physiological response that resets the mind, activating a desired mood. Certain aromas can reduce stress, improve sleep, boost immunity, and soothe headaches.

Scented candles are one way to enjoy the benefits of aromatherapy. Simply light a candle, inhale the fragrance, focus your intention on the desired mood, and experience the effects. To reduce tension, try a jasmine- or lemon-scented candle. Jasmine elevates the mood, and lemon evokes a sense of cleanliness and order. Reduce fatigue with the scent of rosemary or coffee; even a whiff of these scents activates the alert part of the brain. The robust, woodsy aroma of rosemary also aids in memory retention. A looming deadline calls for the focusing scent of rose or the stress-reducing scent of lilac. Activate creative energy for brainstorming sessions with spicy scents like cinnamon or clove. To calm the nerves, light a lavender-scented candle, breathe deeply, and exhale. Lavender is perfect for the end of the workday, when it's time to decompress.

Here's a chart to help you set the scent wherever you're placing your candles.

## MAKING SENSE OF SCENTS

| Desired Mood | Scents |
| --- | --- |
| Cozy | Apple, cinnamon, sandalwood, coconut, clove, vanilla, cedarwood |
| Energized | Peppermint, jasmine, lemon, grapefruit, patchouli, pine, clove, sandalwood |
| Relaxed | Rose, orange, pomegranate, ylang-ylang, patchouli, frankincense, chamomile, clary sage, sandalwood, vetiver |
| Romantic | Lavender, vanilla, ylang-ylang, patchouli, sandalwood, rose, jasmine, fig |
| Productive | Bamboo, cinnamon, eucalyptus |
| Joyful | Bergamot, jasmine, vanilla, tangerine |
| Sleepy | Lavender, chamomile, sandalwood, neroli |

"Smell is a potent wizard that transports you across thousands of miles and all the years you have lived."

—HELEN KELLER

# SCENE

*Your Living Space, Your Relaxing Space, Your Entertaining Space, and Your Work Space*

When arranged in the right locations, candles can enhance your space and everything you do in it. Allowing the elements of a room to complement candles (or vice versa) enlivens a space. For example, you can animate a room by bouncing warm candlelight off reflective surfaces like mirrors or bathwater. Placing candles at varying levels in a house can add intrigue and functional design. As a general decorating rule of thumb, an odd number of candles is more aesthetically pleasing than an even number. Read on for room-specific recommendations.

## *In Your Living Space*

A living room is used for relaxing, entertaining, and recreating, which makes it the most dynamic space in a house and thus the perfect place for arranging candles at the room's focal point. The fireplace and mantel are two great options.

### MANTEL DISPLAYS

Begin your mantel display by creating a focal point with something you'd like to display. Candles can then be used to accentuate your focal point. For example, a well-placed mirror, painting, or houseplant can be the focal point, with candles strategically placed to frame it and add interest. Hurricane candleholders—cylindrical glass holders—can be filled with objects to highlight a mantel's theme. For example, a beach-themed holder can be filled with sand or seashells, whereas a holiday holder might be filled with pine cones or ornaments. For a timeless look, place tapered candles in brass candlestick holders at varying levels. Positioning taper candles close to a wall on an elevated surface lets their light stretch into dark corners.

For optimal candle placement, aim for either an asymmetrical or balanced arrangement. Asymmetrical designs flow well with a contemporary interior space (e.g., a cluster of three candles on one end of the mantel and one candle at the other). A more

balanced look would mean spacing an odd number of objects across the mantel and placing one candle on each end. For safety, only nonflammable objects should be placed in proximity to burning mantel candles.

## FIREPLACE ARRANGEMENTS

To create the illusion of a cozy hearth without firewood, place pillar candles inside the fireplace at varying heights. Tiered pillar candleholders are specifically manufactured for this purpose. Place candles on trays or dishes to avoid having to clean up any wax spills.

To determine the overall visual effect of a candle arrangement, view it from the entrance or seating

area of a room. Adjust the spacing of objects to close up gaps or create different areas of focus.

## MIRROR ARRANGEMENTS

When light plays off multiple reflective surfaces, a romantic ambience is the result. Having fun with mirror placement can turn a somewhat static candle arrangement into a layered experience. Place a mirror underneath a candle setting to create depth in the design. Or position candles in front of a mirror (or multiple mirrors) to add dimension to a room.

*Scents in your living space*

- Cedar
- Sandalwood
- Sea salt
- Fig
- Lavender
- Lily
- Passion fruit
- Magnolia
- Honeysuckle
- Lilac

## *Candle Crafts*

Spruce up any candle to match your décor with some clever DIY projects:

- **Glitter-dipped** candleholders add festive flair.
- For a **spicy scene**, affix cinnamon sticks vertically around an unlit pillar candle.
- **Holiday holders** can be made by placing rosemary sprigs and cranberries in a mason jar, filling it with water, and topping it with a floating candle.

- **Bold botanical** centerpieces can be created by adhering dried, pressed flowers to an unlit pillar candle.

- For a **nostalgic gift**, adhere a photocopied photo to a clear glass candle container.

- Make a **modern design** by wrapping washi tape around tea light tins.

- For your next **tea party**, create DIY candles by pouring wax into pretty teacups.

- For a **fancy flair**, wrap a decorative candle-holder in antique lace.

- Achieve a **rustic look** by wrapping burlap around an unlit candle and securing the burlap with raffia or twine.

"All the darkness
in the world cannot
extinguish the light
of a single candle."

—ST. FRANCIS OF ASSISI

## *In Your Relaxing Space*

Warm candlelight can instantly soften the atmosphere and help you ease into relaxing and rejuvenating. Here are some décor ideas to brighten your bedroom, bathroom, and other relaxing spaces.

### SIDE-TABLE ADORNMENT

Tend a candle garden by arranging candles alongside natural objects like rocks, houseplants, and moss. A miniature ecosystem is the perfect natural addition to any relaxing space because plants purify the air and create a calming feel. Hurricane holders and terrarium containers come in varying shapes and sizes, from geometric domes and cubes

to clear glass vessels. They can be filled with stones, shells, succulents, cacti, moss, and candles at varying levels (but not too close to plants).

## WALL SCONCES

Used as an atmospheric accent, a wall sconce is a romantic addition to a bedroom or bathroom. Secure a sconce to a stud rather than nailing or drilling into only drywall. For safety and to achieve a consistent burn, position a sconce away from flammable objects like window or shower curtains and away from windows or fans, where air movement might make the candle flicker or go out.

## FLOATING CANDLE ARRANGEMENTS

Floating candles can add an unexpected element to any décor, and they provide endless fun for creative experimentation. Clear glass hurricane holders can be filled with branches, petals, shells, stones, sliced citrus, cranberries, ornaments, leaves, ferns, silk flowers, and fresh flowers. Add water, top with a floating candle, and step back to admire the gorgeous effect.

*Scents in your relaxing space*

- Eucalyptus
- Orange
- Lemon
- Pine
- Lavender
- Rose
- Bergamot
- Cedarwood
- Jasmine
- Ginger
- Honeysuckle
- Amber

## Candles Everywhere

Placing candles at different heights around a room can maximize their effects. For example, hang a candle chandelier from the ceiling for romantic overhead lighting. Or suspend a lantern from the ceiling and place a candle inside for a classic feel. Affix wall sconces around the room for soft, peripheral warmth. For a spa-like feel, scatter scented votives or tea lights across a bathroom windowsill or around the rim of a bathtub.

# *In Your Entertaining Space*

Nothing adds flair to a gathering like twinkling candlelight. Candles are an essential part of any party's centerpiece, and they provide peripheral light when arranged artfully around the room.

## CENTERPIECES

For eye-pleasing symmetry, place an odd number of candles in the center of a table. Experiment with candle height and formation. Do the candles look best cascading in height, circling the center of the table and spaced evenly, or clustered in mismatched heights and shapes? Avoid putting tall candles in places where they might obstruct the dinner guests' views of one another or where guests might reach across a table to serve food or pour drinks. Play around with colors. For an elegant table setting, try classic white. For a more romantic mood, try red. Unscented votives are a good option for dining room centerpieces because scents can compete with the aromas of a meal.

## GOBLET ARRANGEMENTS

Stemware is an elegant option for candleholders. Some candleholders are even manufactured to look like stemware. Experiment with the aesthetic effects of candles placed in wineglasses, goblets, martini glasses, or champagne flutes. Put candles directly into the glass. Or to avoid wax cleanup, use floating candles instead. Be sure to position goblet candles in places where they won't get knocked over while entertaining.

## CANDLEHOLDERS AND CANDELABRAS

Candleholders come in a variety of shapes, sizes, colors, materials, and textures. Some are tiered for candles to be positioned at varying heights. Others hold only a single candle or multiple candles in a line. For a simple DIY candleholder, stick a tapered

## *Minimalist versus Maximalist Dining Décor*

A re you drawn to lively, loud design or do you prefer a peaceful, understated effect? Both approaches can be executed with striking results. The style you choose for any occasion is a matter of personal preference.

**Minimalist** design allows space to dominate a room or tablescape. It favors functionality over festiveness. Sparing and uncluttered, a minimalist candle arrangement might use fewer candles, neutral colors, and more geometric candle containers or stands. Use accent colors like greens and yellows.

**Maximalist** design boasts boldness and doesn't shy away from mixing and matching rich colors, different patterns, and a variety of textures. But there's an order to the chaos: each piece is intentional and adds to the overall lavish landscape of a room or table.

candle into an empty wine bottle. Place the bottle on a dish to collect any wax drips. For a vintage look, invest in an antique brass candelabra. More modern candelabras—with artful designs or geometric frames—are also available.

*Scents in your entertaining space*

- Unscented
- Mint (after dishes have been cleared)
- Blackberry (after dishes have been cleared)
- Whiskey (while drinking post-dinner coffee)
- Cardamom or brown sugar (while enjoying dessert)
- Lemon verbena (in the kitchen, during cleanup)

# *In Your Work Space*

In a home office, candles can harness your creativity and help you to de-stress and refocus.

## FOCUSED ARRANGEMENTS

The company of a warm flicker or clarifying scent can focus the mind and increase productivity. Place candles in an appealing, organized pattern in the center of a conference table or at one corner of a home office desk. Clear glass containers or holders in neutral colors have a calming effect. Amber glass provides a warm, modern accent color.

## *How to Safely Incorporate Candles into an Inspiring Home Office*

To reduce fire risk, place candles away from objects like paper, books, curtains, wires, electronics, and office plants. Container candles or travel candles are perfect for a desk because there's no wax spillage to worry about. Keep lit candles in your field of view at all times to make sure they're burning safely—for example, place next to a computer monitor at a safe distance.

## ZEN ARRANGEMENTS

Add tranquility to your place of productivity by artfully arranging your candles with Zen complements. The bob of a floating candle can calm you at your desk. Fill a hurricane holder with smooth stones or lush greenery for a centering effect. Or surround pillar candles with rock cairns or succulents. Bring the calming effect of a forest inside by adding elements of the natural world to your work space.

*Scents in your work space*

- Coffee
- Lemon
- Jasmine
- Rosemary
- Lavender
- Black currant
- Rose
- Lilac
- Pine
- Cedar
- Peppermint
- Cinnamon

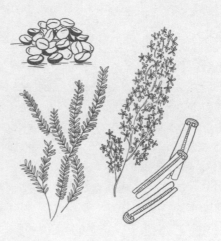

## *Illuminating Event Ideas*

### BIRTHDAY

Match the candles to the cake. For a classy cake decorated with neutral colors, pair it with white or cream candles. Or use candles as an accent color to match the decorations. For children's birthday cakes or themed parties, have fun! Experiment with different colors and shapes. Spell out the person's name in letter candles. If the birthday person has lived multiple decades, use numeral candles for their age (rather than trying to cram fifty candles onto the same cake).

### HOLIDAY

Hurricane holders are perfect for the holidays because they can be filled with holiday-themed foliage and decorations. For example, place a red-berried branch in a clear glass hurricane holder, fill the vessel with water, and top with a floating candle. The red berries add a festive pop of color, and the branches produce elegant patterns in the water. Scented candles make a room feel cozy, filling a space with nostalgic aromas like pine, cinnamon, and citrus. For a woodsy look, pair a container candle with an arrangement of lush greenery like pine, fir, or cedar branches, and then add red accents such as poinsettias, roses, ornaments, or ribbon.

## DINNER PARTY

Low candles are usually best on a dining room table when hosting a dinner party. Tea lights or votives placed in containers with rims taller than the candles will help to prevent exposed flames from interfering with dining activity. Try arranging candles down the length of a table to illuminate the entire spread. Consider hanging mirrors on the wall to help bounce light around the space for an animated atmosphere.

## ILLUMINATING YOUR
# LIFE

---

*Rituals, Candle Magic,*
*Candles in Spirit, and Self-Care*

"Give light, and the darkness will disappear of itself."

—DESIDERIUS ERASMUS

# *Rituals*

Rituals help to set intentions, honor tradition, and instill mindfulness. They ground your practices and prayers. For thousands of years, candles have stirred symbolism and magic into rituals. Scents and colors hold different meanings and add a sense of the sacred. Daily rituals provide reliable points of pause in an otherwise-hurried world. Rituals can also mark milestones throughout a year or over the course of a life.

Rituals are not habits. Habits become so ingrained that they can be executed subconsciously, whereas rituals require full attention. During a ritual, a candle can be used as a temporal marker—the lighting marking the beginning of the ritual and the snuffing out marking the end. For daily rituals, try lighting these candle colors, which align with specific days of the week:

- **Sunday:** gold, orange
- **Monday:** silver, gray, white
- **Tuesday:** autumnal colors like red or brown
- **Wednesday:** gray, yellow
- **Thursday:** purple, blue
- **Friday:** green, pink, brown
- **Saturday:** black

## Candle Magic: Intention-Setting Spells and Symbolism

Candles offer a simple way to incorporate intention-setting spiritual rituals or light magic into your life.

For best results, candle magic should be practiced after the sun has set. First, purify the candle by passing it through the cleansing smoke of sage or incense. Next, you'll want to "charge" the candle—that is, imbue it with your desires. To do this, focus all your attention on the unlit candle and funnel your intention into it. You can also carve a symbol representing your intention into the wax.

Next, anoint yourself—either on the crown of your head or between your eyebrows—with an essential oil that holds the theme of the intention. Incorporate crystals, flowers, stones, tea, and herbs as you see fit. Finally, light the candle; the act of burning links the physical world to the spiritual one—so, don't start a spell that you can't finish.

Align your spell with the cosmos by paying attention to astrological markers. Avoid playing with magic when Mercury is in retrograde. Cast love spells when Venus is in Libra. For new beginnings, wait until the new moon.

In candle magic, a candle's components represent the four basic elements: air, earth, water, and fire. Oxygen fuels the flame. Earth is the candle's solid body of wax. Water is the melting wax, representing fluidity. Fire is the flame.

Notice the flame during any candle spell. A sputtering or popping flame means there might be powers working against you; best to try the spell another time. A blue flame signals that a spirit is nearby. A tall, robust flame means the spell will be successful. A flickering flame signifies the influence of strong feelings on this spell or intention.

Charm your way into more magical living with these beginner candle spells.

## ENERGY INTENTION SPELL
Pick the appropriate color for the intention (see page 40). To draw an attribute toward yourself, carve the word into the candle from the top toward the bottom, and light the candle on the night of a new moon. If you want to draw something out of yourself, write the word from bottom to top, and

light the candle during a waning moon. When lighting the candle, visualize your intention with all your focus, and then blow out the flame. Repeat this process each night until the moon has moved through its waxing or waning cycle. Don't throw away any of the candle's remnants; burn or bury them instead. Don't tell a soul about the spell.

## FOCUS SPELL

To ace your next test or nail your next big work presentation, place a cinnamon-scented blue or yellow candle at your desk as you prepare—blue for wisdom and calm, yellow for concentration and self-assurance. Take a few deep breaths, and then light it up.

## LIFE GOAL SPELL

Choose the right color or combination of colors for your goal. For example, if you want to heal from an illness, use a blue candle (healing) and a black candle (protection). If you want to achieve your life's true calling, select purple (enlightenment) and orange (success). If you want to make money from your creative side hustle, pick orange (creativity) and green (ambition) as your color duo.

Visualize the goal as if you have already accomplished it. Put yourself in the future and imagine the emotions you might feel if you were to attain your goal. Once you can clearly picture yourself succeeding, say your goal aloud. You can sing it, chant it, or turn it into a witchy incantation. When you feel filled up inside by the shining, bright warmth of your goal, light the candle.

Focus on the light emanating from the candle just outside the flame. This is the candle's aura. Imagine the aura expanding through the room, then filling the world, then the universe. Visualize the aura blazing a signal from the universe back to you. Focus on this for as long as you can, until you feel your concentration sputtering out. Then, extinguish the candle.

# Candles in Spirit

Around the world, religions incorporate candles into sacred practices, ceremonies, and holidays. Light is a prominent symbol in many religions, so the candle is a natural vessel for this particular element. Candles help to honor the sacred, bless prayers, and incorporate rituals.

In many cultures, candles are used in memoriam of the dead. They illuminate vigils and shrines. Often, a candle represents the continuation of life after death. The physical body has gone away, but the spirit lives on.

## CHRISTIANITY

Candles represent the light of God or the eternal light of Christ. Votives or tapers are sometimes lit for prayer. Advent wreaths (candles positioned in a circle) are burned in church services in December

on the Sundays leading up to Christmas. On Easter, and during funerals and baptisms, the Paschal candle is lit and represents resurrected Christ. A liturgical candle must be composed of at least 51 percent beeswax in the Roman Catholic Church. In the Orthodox Church, tapers must be 100 percent beeswax.

## HINDUISM

On the new moon day—in the complete darkness of night—Diwali is celebrated by lighting *diyas* (lamps) to ward off evil forces and be rid of selfish thoughts. Diyas symbolize good luck, purity, and power. It is believed that evil forces become more powerful in darkness, so diyas are lit to weaken any dark spirits. The oil in the diya lamps symbolizes moral depravities such as greed, hatred, and jealousy. The cotton in the lamp signifies the human soul or self. Thus, lighting the diya is meant to draw human faults out of the self, pushing humans closer to enlightenment.

## JUDAISM

Throughout the year in Judaism, candles are used to create a calm atmosphere. The lighting of candles takes place during the festivals of Sukkot, Passover, and Shavuot. On Friday evenings, a pair of Shabbat candles are lit to mark the weekly Sabbath celebration. Sabbath is celebrated on Saturday and serves as a day of rest. In Judaism, candles symbolize rest and peace. Memorial candles are lit on the anniversary of the death of a loved one and also on Yom HaShoah, which is a day of remembrance for those who died in the Holocaust.

Hanukkah, also known as the "Festival of Lights," is a Jewish religious celebration that dates back to 165 BC. During Hanukkah celebrations, a candelabrum called a *menorah* is used to honor the rededication of the Temple of Jerusalem. The menorah is the centerpiece of the tradition and holds nine can-

dles. Eight of the candles represent the miraculous number of days the temple lantern blazed, when it only had enough oil to burn for a single day. The ninth candle helps to light the others. During the eight days of Hanukkah, one candle is lit after dark while families recite prayers and sing songs.

## ISLAM

For Muslims, candles symbolize divine light. The Koran is sometimes referred to as "the divine candle." Beeswax candles have contextual significance because honey is described in the Koran as having a heavenly origin. During Eid al-Fitr, an Islamic holiday celebrated after Ramadan (the month of fasting), people light candles around the house to symbolize getting closer to Allah (God).

"Just as one candle lights another and can light thousands of other candles, so one heart illuminates another heart and can illuminate thousands of other hearts."

—LEO TOLSTOY

## BUDDHISM

In Buddhism, candles symbolize respect, deference, or the enlightenment of the Buddha. They're lit before Lent to invite the acceptance of change and impermanence. During the Candle Festival, people parade with candles in colors that symbolize willpower, unity, and the specific beliefs of their community.

## KWANZAA

A kinara holds seven candles for Kwanzaa celebrations, which last from December 26 until January 1. One of Kwanzaa's rituals is the daily lighting of the kinara. On day one, the black candle—or unity candle—is lit, which represents the African American people. On the second day, one of three red candles is lit; the red candles symbolize African American adversity and bloodshed. On day three, one of three green candles is burned; the green candles signify African American hope, future, and abundance. The lighting of the remainder of the candles alternates between red and green on subsequent days.

## DAY OF THE DEAD

Candles symbolize faith and hope during the Day of the Dead. Although originally a Mexican holiday, variations of the Day of the Dead are celebrated throughout Latin America. At midnight on October 31, the gates of heaven open for child spirits to reunite with their loved ones for twenty-four hours. Adult spirits can walk through the gates on November 2 to drink, sing, dance, and feast with their families. During this stretch of time, families honor the dead by gathering in homes and cemeteries; offering candles, food, drink, and marigolds at gravesites; and decorating *ofrendas* (home shrines).

"There are two ways
of spreading light:
to be the candle
or the mirror that
reflects it."

—EDITH WHARTON

## Self-Care

Elevate any self-care ritual with a candle. Adding a candle's soft glow to practices like meditation or tai chi can help to calm the nerves and focus the mind. Animating a room with a gentle flicker can enliven a yoga session or help to unleash creativity and emotions while journaling.

### CANDLE MEDITATION

If you've ever been captivated by the flicker of a fire, you know how transporting a candle's flame can be. Harness this into a mood-lifting candle meditation. Simply lighting candles as you meditate can help set the tone. But candles can do even more when you

make them the center of your meditation practice. Focusing on the flame is grounding for a busy mind and watching fire dance can lull you into a trancelike meditative state. Go one step further by selecting a candle that matches the color of your meditation's intention.

TRY THIS WITH . . .

*Centering, grounding candles:*

- Candle pots
- Pillar candles
- Floating candles

*Soothing, relaxing scents:*

- Vetiver
- Sandalwood

## JOURNALING BY CANDLELIGHT

There's something romantically old-fashioned about writing by candlelight. Just the simple act of lighting a candle before a journaling session can help to focus the mind and funnel creativity onto the paper. You can

## *Five-Minute Candle Meditation*

1. Set up your candle so that it will be at **eye level** during your meditation.

2. **Dim or darken the lights** in the room. Light the candle.

3. Begin by closing your eyes and inhaling deeply to the count of four. Hold it for the count of four, and then exhale to the count of eight. **Repeat three more times.**

4. Open your eyes and **focus your gaze** at the center of the flame. Let your breathing return to normal. Study the fire and empty your mind of all thoughts except this question: What does the flame represent to you?

5. Continue for **at least five minutes** or more.

6. As your meditation time draws to a close, **shut your eyes**.

7. When you're ready, open your eyes and extinguish the flame. **How do you feel?**

use taper candles to set writing goals. Simply mark a point in the wax as your goal line, then write until the candle burns down to that line.

TRY THIS WITH . . .

*Focusing, idea-generating candles:*

- Tapers
- Votives
- Pillar candles

*Scents to spark creativity:*

- Rosemary
- Sage
- Eucalyptus

## YOGA AND CANDLES

Lighting a candle before a yoga session can help put you in the right frame of mind. The presence of a candle can invigorate your Vinyasa flow, circulating the blood and restoring the body's energy reserves. Use a scented candle to incorporate the healing benefits of aromatherapy into your yoga practice. A calming scent can help to relax the mind and find balance in the body during difficult poses.

Also known as *trataka*, candle meditation is one of the six purification techniques of Hatha yoga. Yogis stare at a candle's flame until their eyes water, washing away impurities.

TRY THIS WITH . . .

*Balancing, restorative candles:*

- Votives
- Pillar candles
- Floating candles

*Refreshing, energizing scents:*

- Peppermint
- Grapefruit
- Pine

## OTHER SELF-CARE RITUALS

Light a candle during your morning coffee or tea or while drinking a glass of wine at the day's end. It can also be fun to incorporate a candle into your nightly skin-care routine. Any daily ritual can use a candle to help bring mindfulness to a moment.

"Darkness cannot drive out darkness; only light can do that."

—DR. MARTIN LUTHER KING JR.

# ABOUT THE AUTHOR

Devon Fredericksen is the author of *How to Camp in the Woods* and the coauthor of *50 Classic Day Hikes of the Eastern Sierra*. Her work has been published in *High Country News*, *Yes!*, *Guernica*, and *Indian Country Today*. She earned bachelor's degrees in environmental journalism and Spanish from Western Washington University. She's an amateur beekeeper living in Portland, Oregon, with her husband, cat, and thousands of honeybees.